MW01488872

Thanks to all who encouraged me to write this book and supported me during the most difficult time of my life. And very special thanks to my husband and kids for staying by my side every step of the way. May all the glory go to God for giving me the strength, hope, faith and courage to share my journey.

Chapter 1

Hearing His Voice

In order for you to get a good idea of how my journey started, I need to take you back to May 2010, a couple months before I was diagnosed with breast cancer. There were many moments that came together in order for me to find my cancer and those moments are important to know in order to understand how I made it through my journey.

In May of 2010, I began having some serious pain in my pelvic area and I have a high pain tolerance so for me to say serious pain, it was SERIOUS PAIN! I'm not big on going to the doctor for every little pain but this sent me to the doctor's office without hesitation. I went to my gynecologist and he suspected I had endometriosis in my C-section scar. No problem, this should an easy fix. So the following week I went in for a minor outpatient procedure to remove the abnormal scar tissue that was thought to be causing the pain. The lump was removed and within a few days I was back to my normal routine. When I say normal routine, at that time, for me normal was working eight hours a day, coming home to cook supper and work another two-three hours in my dad's garden. My dad was going through some health issues at the time and since he had already planted his garden and didn't want it to go to waste, he ask us if we wanted to maintain his garden(1-2 acres of garden) until he could resume activity.

Within a couple weeks, the pain returned and this time it was debilitating. I could barely walk, I couldn't work and I could hardly move without cringing in pain. Back to the doctor I went and this time he suspected the endometriosis had spread beyond the c-section scar and going in to take the original lump out irritated the root cause. The verdict: I needed a total hysterectomy. Not what I expected or wanted to hear.

Here it is summertime, my kids are in the middle of baseball season, I'm taking care of my dad's massive garden and I don't have time for a major surgery. I actually told the doctor I didn't know if I could do that right now. He told me to call when I got ready.

I really wrestled with whether to have this surgery or not for about a week. My stubborn self just didn't want to give in and do it. I kept telling myself there was too much going on, not now. I basically argued with myself for a week. Arguing happens to be one of my greatest gifts. That following Sunday is when I argued no more.

I was at church and I was praying very hard about whether I should have the hysterectomy now or wait. I was so reluctant to do it at the time because it was just so inconvenient. During prayer time, I heard this very deep, strong yet gentle voice say, **"WHY WOULD YOU SUFFER MY CHILD?"** I will never forget those words. The voice was so deep and stern but so caring and at the same time the voice was very matter of fact. Like there was no time to waste. Needless to say, it got my attention. I can remember looking up from my prayer time to see who was talking to me and thinking how rude it was to be talking when I was praying. I looked around and everybody around me still had their heads down praying. This voice wasn't coming from just anyone; it was coming from a certain someone! It was at that moment I realized God was speaking to me. Now, before you go and call me crazy, hear me out. I had heard people say God had spoken to them about this and that and I too was never one to really take God speaking directly to someone completely serious. I have always believed He could do anything He wanted; after all He did create the world and everything in it. I suppose speaking to someone directly wouldn't be that hard for Him. I guess I just never thought I would be one that He would speak to directly or indirectly. But He did and I knew it without a doubt. I didn't just hear Him, I felt Him. I knew it was the real deal. No doubts, well at least after I realized I wasn't hearing things and nobody around me was whispering in my ear. Sometimes it takes me a minute or two or maybe a day or two to grasp what is happening right before my eyes. This all happened within about five minutes and in those five minutes, I realized that if God thought it was important enough to speak directly to me then I better make a phone call and get this surgery scheduled. The next day I did just that, I called and scheduled my surgery. I still had no desire to have the surgery because I knew there would be a lot of down time and I simply didn't have time to be down. But I kept telling myself God knows this hysterectomy is important and I must go through with it. I knew enough about God to know when He speaks, you better listen because He will get your attention one way or another. That doesn't always keep me from arguing with Him but He always wins! I'm very thankful He always wins because it seems that when I attempt to do things my way, it always ends in disaster. You see, God can see what we cannot, He can see the bigger picture where we can only see what is right In front of us. There are many things that we would do differently if we could see the big picture. I'm sure just like me, you can think of a few examples in your life that had you been able to see what lay ahead you might not have made that particular decision at that time. I believe God is our eyes to be able to see those things that are ahead, the things that we cannot see and are not intended to see in our flesh. We just have to make a choice to see through His eyes and not our own.

Approximately two weeks after making the appointment to have my hysterectomy, it was done. I had all girl parts removed and after some healing time I would be good to go! So I thought……. it wasn't long after the surgery, I knew different. My troubles were just beginning.

During this time, I did not mention to anyone about hearing His voice. It was something very personal to me plus if I told anyone they would surely think I had lost my mind.

Immediately after the hysterectomy, I noticed a considerable amount of shrinkage in my breast. At first, we made a joke of the shrinkage and we even joked with the dr about not paying for a breast reduction. He said more than likely it was due to changes in hormone levels from the hysterectomy. Honestly, I really didn't care. After all, my breast had served their purpose. Big or small, perky or droopy, I was done with them. They were just extra weight for me.

About three weeks later I had gotten out of the bath tub and as I was drying off, I casually ran my hand over my right breast. When I did, I felt a lump that I was not familiar with at all. It is so important to know your breast. I know that might sound a little weird but if you know them well then you will know when you feel something different. I thought maybe I hadn't noticed it before because of the size difference in my breast. But, at the same time I had the gut wrenching feeling that this was not good. Briefly, I considered ignoring the lump. I mean who wants to go get a lump checked that might be cancer. It's so much easier to just ignore it and hope it goes away right? I knew better though and I had a post hysterectomy check-up in a few days so I convinced myself to ask about it then.

At my check up I brought the lump to the attention of my doctor. Immediately after feeling the lump he made an appointment for me to get a mammogram. Since we were leaving for Virginia in a few days, they were kind enough to work me in the following day. The mammogram showed lots of dense tissue but nothing resembling a tumor. The technician told me that sometimes things can hide under the dense tissue so we were going to look by ultrasound just to be cautious. When the ultrasound was done, the doctor was suspicious of an area about nickel size and decided he wanted to biopsy the area. Let's just say a biopsy was not pleasant but it was necessary and sometimes you just have to do what you have to do to get the answers needed. Within a couple of days, the doctor called and told me what I did not want to hear. The biopsy showed abnormal cells that resembled cancer but they needed the entire lump to know exactly what we were dealing with. The cancer was in a very early stage was the only thing he was sure of at that time. A few weeks later, I had the lump removed by a breast cancer specialist. She called within a day or two with the results and that day I received the most dreaded news. She told me I had stage one cancer which was actually the good news. The bad news was the tissue surrounding the tumor was abnormal and the tumor was a multifocal point tumor. I was told most tumors have one focal point that they grow from and mine had four focal points that it was growing from. That was a bit scary to hear. Then she proceeded to tell me that I would need a mastectomy. I think I was halfway prepared to hear I had cancer but then the doctor started talking about a mastectomy and that it wasn't a matter of **IF** the cancer would come back, it was a matter of **WHEN** because of my age so the best approach to start with was to have a mastectomy. That was the day my world, as I knew it, was gone. I was in for the fight of my life!

The moral to this part of the story is, had I not listened to God's voice that Sunday morning, I believe with all my heart that I would not be writing this book today. When God spoke to me, He was not referring to the hysterectomy at all. He knew I had to go through the hysterectomy to find the lump. Its proof to me and hopefully to you, that God knows what lies ahead for each of us. We just have to learn to listen and not be hearing impaired. He will not lead us astray.

For I know the plans I have for you, says the Lord. They are plans for good and not disaster, to give you a future and hope. Jeremiah 29:11

Chapter 2

Be Strong

Not long after being diagnosed with breast cancer, our pastor preached a sermon regarding David and goliath. Honestly, at the time, my thoughts were all over the place and I was no more paying attention in church than the two year old sitting in the next section over. I was in complete shock for several weeks after receiving the news. In church, I could hear the pastor talking but the words just seem to be flying over my head. Then, all of a sudden, it was like he took a megaphone and screamed, "Strength of David!" Those three words became an anchor for my soul. Just like David, I was fighting my own goliath. I needed the same strength David had in order to fight my battle. For several weeks, I would write **"STRENGTH OF DAVID"** on the palm of my hand. Jesus was nailed to the cross through the palm of His hands so writing those three words on my palm reminded me of what Jesus went through for me. After writing those words on my hand and having to rewrite them over and over, I decided to go permanent and get a tattoo. I had always wanted one but didn't want to get it unless it had meaning. To me, those words and my tattoo would always hold a reminder of what I went through and the strength God blessed me with to get through my journey. On my forearm, is an old rugged cross, draped with a pink ribbon and hovering over the top are the words, "Be strong." By putting it on my forearm, I knew I would be able to see it every day and be reminded that no matter what goliath I face in life, as long as I remain strong like David, I will be victorious!

I can do all things through Christ who strengthens me. Phil 4:13

Chapter 3

The Peace

One night after being diagnosed, I was sitting alone on our trampoline. I spent hours that night crying my eyes out, yelling at God and pleading with Him to explain to me why this was happening. Why did I have to have cancer? Why did my family have to go through this? I questioned Him, I cussed at Him and I was just plain angry at Him that night. I would look up at the stars and think to myself, "You made the stars but **You** can't or won't heal me?" It just made no sense at all to me!

As I sat on our trampoline, I had our little dog with me. Animals are good therapy for every situation. They just love you for loving them. After an hour or two of balling my eyes out, my dog came over and sat in my lap. She was afraid and shaking because she had never been on a trampoline. It was then that I heard His voice (God's voice not the dog's voice). He said to me, "this is exactly how I want you to be towards me in your storm. Come, my child, and crawl into my lap. Let Me wrap my arms around you when you are afraid. Just as you have wrapped your arms around your puppy when she is scared, I will do the same for you and carry you through. I have gone before you and know what lies ahead. Let Me handle all your worries."

After that night of just me, God and my dog, I made a choice to allow God to use me to glorify His name through my storm. I realized that this storm wasn't about me having cancer at all but about what God could do through me during the cancer. From that point on I felt an indescribable peace and strength that could only come from God. There was just no other explanation for what I was feeling knowing I was about to embark on the hardest journey of my life. That doesn't mean what you're going through is going to be a cake walk because I can guarantee it will not but I can guarantee when you allow God to carry those burdens, the path will be much smoother. Lay it all down at the feet of Jesus. That is where you will find peace!!

I have told you all this so that you may have peace in Me. Here on earth you will have many trials and sorrows. But take heart, because I have overcome the world. John 16:33

Chapter 4

Glimpse of His Glory

Although I had found a supernatural peace, the fact remained I did have cancer and there was a process to being healed. I remember driving home from work one afternoon, crying my eyes out yet again. I was crying so hard I had to pull over. When I parked the car, I just threw up my hands and yelled, **"WHY CAN'T YOU JUST HEAL ME RIGHT NOW?"** I went on to explain to God that I was worthy of an instant healing. That we had a great relationship and I was a regular church attendee. I explained to Him how much I loved Him and how I try so hard to live for Him. Here I was pleading my case like He didn't already know it all. I was like a kid in the store trying to explain to my parents why I needed candy or whatever. I knew God healed spontaneously in certain situations but I just couldn't understand why **I** couldn't be one of those "Jonny on the spot" healings. Why did I have to suffer? Why did my family have to suffer? Why? Why? Why? I needed an answer! I felt as though God owed me an answer. After all that was the least He could do if I was going to go through breast cancer and glorify His name. At least in my mind I thought that was only fair. Of course He did not owe me anything but my flesh was front and center so I was making lots of demands that I didn't deserve. As I look back on that moment, I picture God sitting patiently and quietly with His hands folded together shaking His head in agreement, not saying a word. Basically, just listening to me rant as though He knew what I was going to say before I said anything. He always does know because He has already been there and He can see the bigger picture.

Believe it or not, He gave me my answer within a couple of days of my little meltdown. He is faithful in His word. His timing and ours do not always coincide but His word is faithful. I had been going to church every morning to pray. It was awesome! Many mornings it was just me, God and worship music. One particular morning, I was laying face down praying and I heard His mighty voice. It's one of those voices that you know who it is when you hear it. Plus, I had heard it before so I was very familiar by this time. I still had to look up to see who was talking to me, like I didn't know already. God said to me, **"GO GET YOUR**

BIBLE." The funny thing is, I never carried my Bible to prayer but for whatever reason on this day I carried my Bible. I was being obedient before I even knew to be obedient. There was just something that morning that told me I would need my bible. Do you think maybe a little Holy Spirit directing my steps? Yes, I think so. After being instructed to "go get my Bible", I walked to the back of the sanctuary to get my Bible. I had no idea what I was going to do with it when I opened it but I knew that He would show me eventually. As I picked it up, He told me to open to Romans 8:17 which reads, *"Now if we are His children, then we are His heirs-heirs of God and co-heirs with Christ, if indeed we share in His sufferings in order that we may also share in His glory."* WOW! Did you read that? Do you remember earlier in the chapter my specific question? Why do I have to suffer? I found my answer in that verse. Once again, His word is faithful. My answer was written thousands of years ago; He led me right to the verse, word for word. All of our answers are right there in one book. I ask for an answer and I got an answer. He always has an answer to our questions. We have to be patient and wait on Him to show us the answer. We have to listen and be observant. Not all answers are going to be in the form of words. Many times He uses actions, dreams, sermons, people and objects to deliver His answer. **WE** have to learn to observe our surroundings. He is constantly speaking to us and He is everywhere and can do anything! It may not be in our time and it may not be how we want it to be but He knows best.

After reading Romans 8:17, I was floored at the thought that God thought enough of me to allow me to experience a tiny bit of the suffering that His son Jesus had endured. Of course my sufferings were nothing compared to what Jesus experienced. We could never endure the pain and suffering that He was subjected to. We were not made to suffer as Jesus suffered. God sent His son to absorb all of it for us and that is a prime example of true love. It was then that I realized that regardless of how my journey ended, I would be fine. I knew that God would provide the strength I needed and carry me all the way through. That's exactly what he did and I don't think my feet touched the ground from that moment on. As you read this, keep in mind that these sorts of moments don't just appear out of nowhere. It isn't this elaborate magical moment with stardust raining down. These moments of hearing God's voice and understanding His plan are choices that I made along the way. I could have easily ignored everything and chalked it up to me being crazy. I'm not saying I'm not crazy because anyone who knows me will verify there is a little craziness that follows me. I made choices to be obedient, to listen for His voice and to try to understand His plan for me. We have the right to choose which path we take. God does not force us to see things His way and only His way.

In my case, I knew my cancer was far more than I could handle alone. Don't get me wrong, I was and still am very blessed with a wonderful supportive family, circle of friends and church family. They were all a tremendous help and I could not have ask for better but honestly, it just wasn't enough. I'm not meaning that in a bad way but when you go through a battle of this magnitude you better find some spiritual strength!! You have to learn to recognize the times when you as a person, need more than any human can provide. In the flesh, we are very limited in our ability to fix certain things. Well, frankly, we are limited to whatever God has decided our limitations are as human beings. If we didn't have limits as to what we are capable of doing then we wouldn't need God. He designed us to need Him for a reason!

For God called you to do good, even if it means suffering just as Christ suffered for you. He is your example and you must follow His steps.
Peter 2:21

Chapter 5

Let's do this!

After finally coming to grips with the fact that I had cancer, I was ready to move forward. I was ready to start the process so I could reach my destination. When I came to grips, I learned to focus more on the finish line than focusing on the starting block. This a much better approach especially when the race could be long and tough. In the beginning it feels as though time is standing still but your surroundings are moving in every direction. It seemed very chaotic! I can remember during this time, I would watch people and think to myself, "They are just walking across the parking lot like nothing is wrong." They were going on about their normal lives and here I was battling cancer! I'll admit I was a little jealous at times. But that was just satan trying to get into my head. You don't ever know what others might be experiencing. It may not be what you are facing but what they are facing could be just as devastating to them as cancer was to me. I would think about how I knew people who deserved cancer far more than I did. That is what I thought anyway. I had to sort of slap myself back into focus at times. Nobody, not even your worst enemy deserves cancer and I really didn't wish that on anyone. From time to time I would leave a tiny crack open just enough for satan to sliver his way into my thoughts. My heart however was occupied by Jesus. I would just tell myself to **FOCUS, FOCUS AND FOCUS**! I had to continuously remind myself to focus. It was a full-time job to stay on track and not let satan put up road blocks. There wasn't a minute that satan didn't try to take me down.   First of all, I wasn't being punished regardless of satan's lies. Secondly, nobody deserves cancer or any other illness or discouraging situation anymore than another. Instead, I chose to believe God picked me for the job because He had confidence in me that I could do it. He knew I could handle this job. The way I see it, everybody has a job to do for God. Most of the time, it's just a matter of taking the time to recognize that is what is going on in our lives. It's so easy to fall into the pit of self pity when life is tough. When life is good, we are good. It's human nature to be that way. Yes, we are human but we have capabilities far beyond what we could ever imagine for ourselves. Someone died for us humans so we could reach way down deep when life isn't so good. When life is good for us but not others, we can reach way down deep for that person. God equipped us to do not only for ourselves but for others going through rough waters. We see super heroes on television and think to ourselves, "that can never happen." Well, most things we see on television involving super heroes aren't possible and if they were are beyond our capabilities. But we have a superhero in heaven who has given us the same superpowers that He uses. The supernatural abilities that we possess may not spit webs from our wrist or move buildings with one hand but He has blessed us to heal people, experience supernatural peace and strength that allow us to weather the storms we endure. If it makes you feel better, put a cape printed with a big G on your back and proclaim your super hero to be God!

I had a lot to do to prepare for surgery and treatments. I had to prepare my home and family for what was to come. I knew once it all started, I would be down for a while. Everybody knows when mom is down, everything around the house tends to suffer a bit. Nothing against the men in the house, it's just a woman thing. The microwave gets overused as does the dishwasher and the vacuum cleaner maybe not so much; anyway, you get my point. I will admit, my family and friends were beyond great in helping with those chores. My pre-appointments and prep test came and went without any problems. Thank goodness because I already had enough problems with the booby cooties. Finally, my surgery date had come. The beginning of my long, rough, uphill battle had begun. September 9, 2010 is a day etched in my mind forever. How do you prepare for something so life altering? Well, you don't and you can't, you just take one day at a time and pray for the best. Just a month ago, I was preparing to leave for Virginia. Now here I was lying in the surgery holding area not knowing what the next year would bring or even if I would be around to see the next year.

The morning of September 9, was a somber one. We got up early and left before dawn. It was about an hour drive so we basically sat in silence for an hour. In my hand was a gold cross that I had been clutching since I got out of bed that morning. I clutched that small cross with every ounce of strength I had right up until they took me back for surgery. It was my way of depending on Jesus to get me over the first hurdle. It seemed like forever from the time we left the house until the time they completed my surgery preparation. There was a lot of prep involved, from disinfecting to sharpie lines all over my chest. I'm ticklish so drawing on my chest was entertaining for everyone. When the time came to take me back, they let all of my family back to say goodbye. There were a lot of people in that small room on that morning. It was a very emotional few minutes. Even as I write about it now I still have tears in my eyes. I'm thankful for all the support of family and friends. I know none of this was easy for them but they were there for me in many different ways. The time came for me to leave for surgery; my husband still by my side leaned down to kiss me and said "I love you." I returned the gesture, handed him that cross and told him to hold onto it because there is power in the cross!

Eight hours later I came out of surgery a whole new woman. I was miserable to say the least but thankful because I knew I had a huge step behind me, which means I was one step closer to the finish line. God was still in control and leading my journey.

No wonder my heart is glad and I rejoice. My body rests in safety. Psalms 16:9

Chapter 6

Getting Stripped

Once I fully awakened from the anesthesia after my mastectomy, I thought surely I had died! My chest felt like someone had performed CPR and used a rib spreader. Needless to say that anxiousness I felt to get started had turned into,"oh no what was I thinking!" I had drain tubes hanging from the front, back and sides. There was nasty junk flowing through the tubes and the pain was unimaginable!! I had no idea what I had gotten myself into and I'm thankful I didn't know before the surgery because it would have been easy to back out knowing what I knew afterwards.

After a couple days of recovering from the worst surgery ever, it was time for the one hour trip home. Believe me, I felt every crack, pothole and rock on the interstate to home. That was by far the most uncomfortable ride home. I didn't physically jump out of the car when we got home but mentally I was moving at leaps and bounds to get away from that car. Me, cars and bumps did not get along for quite a while! However, I, the couch and the bed did become very close! Like BFF close!!

It was a difficult transition for me post surgery. I went from being an active, healthy 37 year old woman with three kids' pre surgery to being a useless, needed 24/7 care scarred woman with cancer all in about a month's time. I lost all modesty and felt completely helpless. I couldn't use my arms for almost a month for anything other than eating and drinking. I always needed someone with me to help me up, bath me and wash my hair. I had never pictured myself being in such a needy situation. I was always the helper not the helped.

So here I was in a predicament that I had to totally depend on someone else to make it through a day. I had to surrender all of me to whoever was there at that moment. Sound familiar? Not only had I surrendered all of who I was to God, I had to surrender all of who I once was as a mother, wife and woman to another human being. Dignity was way out the door! But by this time, I had learned that God had His way of completely stripping you of who you once were to be the person He wants you to be. Just when you think you couldn't possibly be stripped of anything else, He will strip another layer from you. There is always a little more we can be stripped of in order to be humbled. He wasn't done stripping me either!! It actually felt good to be stripped of so much stuff. It was allowing me to feel more of Him.

So be truly glad. There is wonderful joy ahead, even though you have to endure many trials for a little while. 1 Peter 5:7

Chapter 7

Time for Bigger Boxing Gloves

A month after I thought it couldn't get any worse....chemo started! I had no idea a person could feel that bad and still be alive. I understand why people want to give up when going through that mess. I'm not saying I wanted to give up but I certainly understood the logic behind the thought. The first 3 days after treatment were the worst. I didn't care how much I drooled because I was just too tired to swallow. After the 3rd day, I would begin to feel somewhat better. As good as you can feel after a horrendous surgery and poison running through your veins. Just when things started to look up, the bottom falls out. I began to run fever and the thing you want to do while on chemo is run fever. I had the chills that I'm sure burned thousands of calories. I had never shaken like that in 37 years. My blood pressure was dangerously low and I wasn't regenerating red cells so my hemoglobin was very low. All that made for one sick lady. At that point I found myself back in the hospital and in isolation. Isolation meant no visitors and I was certainly feeling isolated by this time. When you're in the hospital the one thing you look forward to is having visitors so when you can't have those either you become kind of grouchy. The same two people can only look at each other for so long without developing a complex. As tired as you get of looking at each other, there is much comfort in knowing that person is with you. It's sort of an unspoken comfort. You do snap at each other and sometimes wish you could see a different face for a change but deep in your heart you know you couldn't do it without those certain people.

After treating me a few days with antibiotics, I wasn't getting better, I was only getting worse. I finally got up to take a shower and when I did I knew exactly what the problem was and I immediately told my nurse. One of my new boobs was very red and swollen.......it was infected. Not only did my first pair try to kill me, now my second pair was after me fast and in a hurry!

After talking to all necessary personal, it was determined I needed emergency surgery to remove the implants that had been used in reconstruction. Can you guess who fell into the 10% of those who might reject the man made tissue used for reconstruction? You got it, yours truly. The only problem was I needed a blood transfusion before I could have the surgery. Plus I had to be transferred back to the hospital that put the implants in which was 60 miles away. I was truly in the middle of a hot mess.

At this point, there was nothing left to do but have a total meltdown. That is exactly what I did but only for a few minutes. I sat right in the middle of my hospital bed and cried like a baby in my husband's arms. After about 15 minutes, I just stopped, like turning a faucet off. I looked at my husband and said, "Ok, that's enough! At this point, we just have to put on bigger boxing gloves because the bigger the fight, the bigger the boxing gloves. My battle just got bigger and so did my boxing gloves.

Sorry devil, I'm tag teaming with God and He just tagged in an extra load of courage and strength!! You see, sometimes we feel as though the devil keeps piling it on and we get weary because the load is so heavy. As if it wasn't bad enough that I was fighting cancer after a major surgery, now I'm facing another surgery to remove any progress. One step forward and 10 steps back. I felt as though I was losing this race. It makes you so very weary at times and that is normal. That is when we need to be reminded we are not fighting this battle alone. The Lord will carry us through whatever we ask him to carry us through. He is there for us always. We have to make the effort to lay our burdens at His feet so that He can carry that burden or help us carry that burden. When Jesus carried His cross to Calvary, He laid the foundation for us to be able to lay our troubles down at the cross. It's about us making a choice to do so.

Don't be afraid, for I am with you. Don't be discouraged, for I am your God. I will hold you up with my victorious right hand. Isaiah 41:10

Chapter 8

Bald and Beautiful

To some, being a young bald woman with a flat chest is to say the least, horrifying. But I've never been one to focus much on looks. Don't get me wrong, I've always done my hair and wore make up, mainly to keep from scaring the snot out of people, but never can I be accused of wearing too much make-up or overdoing the hair. Now, here I was as natural as natural could be and it didn't bother me at all. But what must my husband think? I can't possibly be attractive to him. Those were just a few of my thoughts and fears as I looked at my reflection. He wasn't looking at my outer beauty or lack of; he always looked inward at my heart. I caught him staring at me one day and immediately got defensive. I said, "What are you staring at?" His reply, "I've never seen you look so beautiful. Your eyes are so beautiful!" My husband was looking at me through God's eyes not his flesh eyes. When we look at things through God's eyes everything looks and is beautiful.

After the emergency surgery, I decided to focus more on treating the cancer than reconstruction because reconstruction did me no good if I couldn't beat the cancer. Not long after arriving home from the last surgery, I was looking at my reflection in the mirror. I had no hair because while I was hospitalized it had started falling out from the first chemo treatment. As my eyes lowered to my chest, I just stared at how flat it was since everything had been removed. I had tubes and scars everywhere. But as bad as I felt like I looked on the outside, my inner self was screaming, "**YOU HAVE A STORY TO TELL!**" That thought became my driving force to write about my journey in hopes of helping others who are going through something. It doesn't have to be cancer that a person is going through. It can be anything because we all have something to battle. I have spoken at different small functions over the past few years and each time I tell my story a little differently because there are so many different directions that one can deliver their journey. I feel that my battle is someone else's strength. That goes for everyone because someone else may be fighting a different battle that can help you get through your battle. God wants us to use our battles to reach others who are going through their own battle. It's not so much about what causes the battle as it is how you fight the battle.

God didn't choose us to fight these battles to remain silent. He chose us so we could be the light for someone else who might be lost in the dark. Go tell what God has done in you so that others can gain the strength they need to fight and then hopefully pass along the light to someone else in a way that it will continue to inspire others who need hope.

Instead, you must worship Christ as Lord of your life and if someone asks about your Christian hope, always be ready to explain it. 1 Peter 3:15

Chapter 9
Moving Right Along

Thankfully, I was able to resume chemotherapy in November 2010. The more complications that arise during treatments and the more treatments are postponed, the longer it takes to get finished. I can remember trying to plan my treatments around the holidays. Chemotherapy really messes with your taste buds so I wanted to be able to taste the yummy food and feel descent. At Thanksgiving, I was truly thankful for many things but I was so very thankful for being able to taste the awesome food cooked by my mom and mother-in-law. Its bad when you can smell food, crave the food, only to be able to not to taste the food. It's a terrible disappointment. My taste buds still act up from time to time but it usually subsides within a week or two and it's not nearly as bad as when I was taking treatments. I can remember eating a five gallon bucket of red hot candy because that's all I could taste. Chicken tasted like paper (not that I've eaten paper) but you know, sometimes you just know. I also had a friend at Sonic who would make sure I had a cherry coke waiting at the drive thru when chemo was over. I don't know why I craved cherry coke after chemo but it was amazing!! It's just little things like tasting food, red hot candy and cherry cokes that made the journey a little sweeter.

Once I had the implants removed and restarted treatments it was basically smooth sailing. There were good days and bad days but the good days are there to remind you of how bad the bad days can be. I wasn't able to work because I was so susceptible to germs and I worked in healthcare so working just wasn't an option. I missed working like crazy and it would have kept my mind busy but it was for the best. I mostly stayed home, watched movies and did a lot of praying. I, my 2 dogs, the couch and God had lots of bonding time. The quiet time was a time that enhanced my spiritual life abundantly. I wouldn't have traded that time for anything. Yes, many days I felt horrible physically but spiritually I felt so alive!! I miss those days where I had all the time in the world to pray and spend time in His presence. I still do spend time praying and in His presence but with life's responsibilities it feels so limited. I don't feel good about limiting my time with God because I know He doesn't limit himself with us. I know He understands though. I can tell you that the answers to life and how to deal with any situation lies in spending time in His presence. It helps to read the word and pray tremendously but spending that time with Him is essential to survival. I lived both ways and can testify as to the difference in spending time with Him and not spending time with Him. That principle goes along with anything in life. If you want to grow in whatever you're doing or facing you must spend time with that which you are experiencing. That includes things like marriage, friendship, work, school, spiritual life and even yourself. We cannot grow as humans if we don't spend time with ourselves. As a matter of fact, in a sense, I have told my middle son that same thing many times. You must love yourself and who you are before you can know what love feels like or before you can love anything else.

There were no more problems throughout the next few months as I continued chemotherapy and for that I was thankful. I felt like I had encountered enough problems thus far to last a lifetime. Something can always be learned from each trial we face on a daily basis. It usually comes down to us making the choice whether to learn or not learn.

Rejoice in confident hope. Be patient in trouble and keep on praying. Romans 12:12

Chapter 10

The New Normal

In February of 2011, I finished the "rough stuff" chemotherapy. I remember walking out of the Drs. Office that day thinking, "I'm free! I can have my life back now!" Boy was I wrong. The life I knew before cancer was gone, plain and simple. I learned real fast that I would never be that person again. Some of that was good and some not so good.

I waited a month before returning to work part-time. I thought waiting a month was a good time frame. I kept thinking, "If I can just go back to work, I will be good. Everything will be back to normal." Again, I was wrong. Wrong about a month after treatment being long enough, wrong about going back to work making things normal again, I was just wrong about a lot that first year post chemo. Going back to work that soon slowed my healing process down. My body had been basically tortured for a year so it needed way more than a month to heal. Even though it was only part-time it took a major toll on me physically which drained me emotionally and mentally. I've often said the hardest time for me was afterwards when I was trying to find my new normal. Most days I worked, I would work a few hours and go home only to go to bed. The bed is the last place I wanted to be because I had spent almost a year laying down. That's when I realized, I had a whole new battle in front of me. Once again, I found myself experiencing a little bit of anger because I wanted to feel whole again and felt as though I deserved to feel whole again because I had given up almost a year of my life to cancer. I still had the reconstruction to go through. Yes that was my choice and I don't regret it because that was part of me being able to feel whole again. The cancer took something, a lot of "somethings" away from me and I wanted them back. I didn't realize there was so much healing time needed post chemo. I didn't even give my mind or body a chance to heal. I thought I did but my thinking wasn't in the right mind frame. I don't remember anyone saying that it was going to take this long or that long for your body to heal. Everybody is different in their healing process but I'm certain a month isn't enough time for any of them. I set a time limit on myself and epically failed. My advice is to not set a time limit for anything regarding healing time during and after cancer. I resorted back to the "one day at a time "method.

The reconstruction was a staged surgery meaning the surgery had to be done in three different stages or three different surgeries. Have a surgery, let it heal, have a surgery, let it and have another surgery. By this time and after five plus surgeries, I should have been able to do my own surgery. Each surgery took its toll on my body physically but I was able to bounce back quicker each time. My body was finally getting stronger. It was a slow process but everything in life is a process. We have to give things a chance to process out and not expect everything to turn out how we want it or when we want it.

Finally, sometime in January 2012, I was able to resume work as a full time employee. Was it too soon again? Probably but you don't know until you try. I worked miserable for ten months. On my lunch break, I would go to my car and lay down for 30 minutes. I could have lain there the rest of the afternoon but 30minutes was enough to get me through until five o'clock so I could go home and lay down the rest of the night. The morning would come and I would drag myself out of bed and back to work. I felt like my butt was still at home by the time I was clocking in at work. Always felt like I was just dragging behind. After about ten months of that I finally said, "I did not beat cancer to live a dead life." It was time to make a decision as to whether I could continue working or give into the fatigue and stay home. As you have probably concluded by now, I am somewhat stubborn so I decided to visit my doctor for some help. I just wasn't ready to give in to the fatigue. Once again this is part of a process and not the end so I wanted to look at every available option to me that would help me through the process. I knew God hadn't abandoned me but I was trying to do things my way. My way, your way, well, they are not God's way and I believe that if you live for God then its best you let Him do things His way because He can see the bigger picture that we cannot see. There are a lot of things we would do differently if we could see what God sees. That is why it is important to seek His counsel in all situations. Does that mean you will make every right decision? Absolutely not but it will be much easier to see things through God's eyes if you seek Him first.

And I am certain that God, who began the good work within you, will continue his work until it is finally finished on the day when Christ returns. Philippians 1:6

Chapter 11

Making Changes

Not long after I had had enough of the fatigue, I saw my Oncologist. I ask him, "Is this it? Is this how my life is going to feel after beating cancer?"

My heart sank when he said, "Probably, you're almost a year out of treatment and that's about the length of time it takes to reach your peak." He went on to explain everyone is different in how their body heals from chemotherapy. Some take a little longer than others. I felt a little better knowing I could just be lagging behind a little. But I couldn't accept being so tired all the time just doing normal everyday things. My mind just kept thinking, "This can't be it. It can't be all there is after all I've been through." Not fair! I needed my body to give more. I had things to do, kids to raise and places to go. I didn't beat cancer to still feel so bad. I guess the dr saw my desperation and introduced me to a medicine that helps with fatigue. It was actually a medicine used to treat a sleeping disorder. I was reluctant because I didn't want to take any more meds. I also felt if I couldn't do it without meds then it's wrong. My, my how satan tries to destroy us by telling us lies. I was out of options. It was either try the medicine or go home and become best friends with the couch. I researched the medicine and found that it was a very safe regimen. The next day I started the medicine and within 48 hours was feeling so much better. You may be asking yourself, "If it helps why hesitate to try it?" Well, it's a cancer thing really. You take what you have to take to beat cancer and when you have an option to take more meds you become timid because of all the side effects. For every drug there is a side effect and believe me those side effects can be worse than the disease. Then you have to take something for the side effects so it's a never-ending cycle. But once again, you don't know until you try. I was in a situation to either try it or be miserable. My oncologist always said we are going to swing the biggest bat we have to beat this. Do all we can do so we don't give ourselves the opportunity to look back and say, "If I had done this or that maybe it would have been better?" Go ahead and do all you can now because you don't want to look back with any regrets. That doesn't mean you will succeed at everything you do but it does mean you did everything you could to do what's best.

And we know that God causes everything to work together for the good of those who love God and are called according to his purpose for them. Romans 8:28

Chapter 12

The New Me

Don't get me wrong, I still have days, weeks and sometimes months where I feel like I've been hit by a train. If the fatigue cycle last long enough (which it has been short lived and occasional for about six months now) I begin to question whether I can continue to work. Sometimes I feel like I am going to have to choose between work and family because at times my body just won't allow for both. At this point I can still wiggle my way through the tough days. It's not easy by any means on some days but with God on my side it's much more tolerable as is anything with God on your side. The fatigue cycles are much farther apart and resting actually does help at this point. I hate the fact that I have to resort to resting for my body to catch up but resting is much better than the alternative and there was a time when resting didn't help. So, as times goes on my body improves and that is what I have to focus on more than the fatigue itself. We can get focused on the wrong thing and that too will make us more tired physically, mentally and emotionally. It's very easy to get focused on the wrong things but when you have God you have an advantage of seeing things with totally different eyes… God's eyes. Some days I still push my body too far and usually pay the consequences but I'm learning my limits. I'm getting better about taking one day at a time and listening to my body sooner. I just tend to rebel from time to time. I don't always like who I am physically since the cancer because I do not like limitations. The reality of the situation is that I am a cancer survivor. Being a survivor of anything requires change, acceptance, strength and courage to do what needs to be done to win the war.

Then Jesus said to the disciples, "Have faith in God. I tell you the truth, you can say to this mountain, may you be lifted up and thrown into the sea" and it will happen. But you must really believe it will happen and have no doubt in your heart. I tell you, you can pray for anything and if you believe that you've received it, it will be yours. Mark 11:22-24

Chapter 13

Let Your Light Shine

Many of us find ourselves walking in darkness through our journey. I think that is pretty normal for most of us when we are going through the biggest storm of our life. It's easy to be blinded by darkness when you can't see the light because of your circumstances. You may be asking yourself, "How can you be blinded by darkness?" Sometimes darkness can be totally debilitating because you feel there is no way out. It's as if you are wearing a blindfold in a dark room. There were many days during my journey with breast cancer that I could not see the light much less feel like looking for the light. But God never failed to show me the light in every day. Whether it be looking up at the night sky and seeing the stars or just reminding me my journey is temporary by showing me someone else's situation. Never forget, there is always someone worse off than you. Did you know your situation can be a light for someone else? It's kind of like this: if you see someone who is going through a much more difficult time than you are then it reminds you that it could be worse therefore giving you that little bit of hope that you need to see the light in your storm. The same works for someone who may not be going through what you are but that person is really down and drowning in darkness as they walk through their journey. Then, they see you or talk to you and your light shines in a way that they are able to see that ray of hope. It's a chain reaction just like dominoes toppling over. Only we aren't falling down, we are lifting each other up using our circumstances. I can remember walking down the center isle at my church one Sunday morning and I could just feel every eye in the church upon me. Just the thought of so many people staring at me was a little creepy. Then, the Lord brought it to my attention that these people were not looking at me; they were looking at my light, His light! His light was shining through me and I didn't even know it at the time. Once I realized it, I was in awe of what He was doing through me. He can do the same for you during your storm. It doesn't matter if its cancer, addiction, abuse, or depression, no matter what you're going through God can use it for good!!

You are the salt of the earth: but if the salt has become tasteless, how can it be made salty again? It is no longer good for anything, except to be thrown out and trampled underfoot by me. "You are the light of the world. A city set on a hill cannot be hidden; nor does anyone light a lamp and put it under a basket, but on the lamp stand, and it gives light to all who are in the house. "Let your light shine before men in such a way that they may see your good works, and glorify your Father who is in heaven." Matthew 5:13-16 (NASB)

Chapter 14

Never Give Up

Do you ever have those days when you just want to throw in the towel? Don't worry because you are certainly not alone. Every one of us have that day or for some its multiple days where we say we are done. We say we can't handle another day like this. We become weary with our circumstances and our flesh starts to take over. Before you know it you've fallen into a deep pit of pure muck. Muck is defined as dirt, trash or waste matter. Needless to say it's a deep, dark hole of bad stuff. Spiritually speaking muck could be said to be a dry, dark place that is thick with sadness and hopelessness.

In the beginning of your battle, you have this adrenaline rush that sustains you for a short period of time. It's part of an emotional roller coaster when you're faced with something that is life altering. You have no idea which direction to go because so many things are changing so fast. Your mind is racing from one minute to the next and your physical body is trying to keep up with the demands of the situation. It works for a while and for some people it works longer than for others. But we are so consumed with the newness of what we face that our spiritual being along with our physical body wears down and we lose our sense of meaning and direction. Think about this: if you're wondering around in the middle of nowhere and every direction you turned leads to a dead end, you're going to get tired of running into that same dead end. When we get tired and weary we are more susceptible of falling off the right path. Sometimes when you're in the middle of nowhere and you lose your way because of fatigue and weariness you might land in quicksand. What happens in quicksand? You start to sink, slowly but surely you fall deeper and deeper into this muck that keeps you from moving forward or anywhere except down. If we find ourselves trapped in this pit and we give up all together we will eventually sink all the way to the bottom. The difference in a pit of quicksand and an emotional/spiritual/mental pit of muck is we can get out of the emotional/spiritual/mental pit. It isn't easy by any means but we are blessed enough to have the option to call upon on Father in heaven for help.

Our bodies and our minds are not meant or equipped to handle long, physical, mental and emotional battles alone. God has made available His word, prayer and other believers to help support us during such times. We will all land in that pit at one time or another but it's important not to take up permanent residence there because there is absolutely nothing good at the bottom of that hole. When you feel like you've hit that bottom remind yourself there is one way out and that's up. Use whatever means necessary to get out. Call a friend, pick up the bible or drop to your knees and call out to God. Sometimes it may take all three of those actions and then some to bring you out of that deep dark pit. For me, there were several occasions I found myself sinking deeper and deeper. When you're down and out it doesn't take much at all to fall over that edge. We need a strong foundation and support system to stay upright. We need that even when we aren't going through awful things. If we don't have that then many times our flesh turns to unhealthy habits to cope with our circumstances. Those unhealthy habits lead to destruction and destruction leads to death.

I remember a specific day during my journey that I was particularly weary. I had zero energy, physically, mentally or emotionally. I was literally lying in bed on my side staring into nothing. As I was lying there I could only think about how I couldn't do this anymore. The chemotherapy was taking its toll on me. I started to mumble there is power in Jesus, there is power in Jesus, I mumbled that phrase over and over until I fell asleep. The next morning I woke up to find much of my energy had been restored. There were many days that were just like those days. Some were me just existing spiritually and others came with the whole package. I'm sure as you read this you're agreeing that you have those days as well. Guess what? Those weary days are okay and good to have occasionally. But who wants to have weary, hopeless days? None of us do but we know they are going to come at some point. Some of those days will turn into weeks and some may turn into months. Even though our physical, mental and emotional bodies are weary, our spiritual body can thrive. That is the exact thing that kept me going when the rest of me could not continue. Being weak or weary in those three areas is not a total loss because I feel when we are weak in those three areas our spiritual body has a great opportunity to grow in leaps and bounds. It's like when you can peel those three layers off or remove them from the equation, our spiritual body has room to actually work within us. It's like our spirit can breathe because all that other junk isn't choking us.

It's okay to be broken and it's ok to fall in that pit. Many times we think we are worthless once we are broken or once we fall into that muck but that is farthest from the truth. Those are opportunities for us to learn who we are and what we are capable of doing. It's a great opportunity to see how deep we can reach into our soul for spiritual strength. You yourself may not be able reach as deep as you need to but I can promise if you look hard enough there is someone or something around you that can extend to the depth that you cannot reach. When we use the mercy and grace that surround us we are not only being blessed but we are blessing others. There is something to be learned and taught during every situation. So, instead of letting our situation smother us from every direction, take control of your attitude in that situation and never give up! How do you never give up when the situation seems hopeless? Start by praying, then pray some more and when you feel like you can't pray anymore, keep praying. God hears each and every word we pray. That doesn't mean He will answer us exactly when and how we want but He will answer in His way and His time. Keep a watchful eye and keen ears so that you do not miss His works.

Always pray and never give up. Luke 18:1(NLT)

Epilogue

Hearing the phrase, **"YOU HAVE CANCER"** is one of the most discouraging moments of anyone's life. However, if you remove the "dis" and the "ing" from the word, you are left with courage. Every battle we endure regardless of the size and content can be molded into a journey of growing faith, hope, strength and courage. We always have a choice as to whether we let the battle define us or whether how we fight the battle defines us. Personally, I wanted people to be able to say my name and in the same breath say, "she sure did fight cancer with a lot of courage and faith." Being sick or hurt doesn't mean you can't be a light for Jesus. It means just the opposite, **YOU CAN BE MORE OF A LIGHT FOR JESUS** because you draw more attention during a struggle. I've found that when a person is going through something, people have a tendency to put you in the spot light. God can use you and that spotlight to teach those around you His good works when things life are tough. We can use that spotlight to bring people to Jesus or we can use that spotlight as a negative influence. It's once again a choice we have to make. I think we all want to teach something positive or at least we should. I realized approximately a quarter of the way through my journey that through cancer, God could use me to make a difference in someone else's life. I didn't have to drown in self pity. That person or the people who you touch may not have cancer. Their battle may be addiction, abuse, divorce, anger etc. It doesn't matter the battle that's being fought because they are all opportunities to adapt and overcome. Opportunities to see God's work first hand. Your battle or your struggle can become someone else's hope. It's a time during which you can use your most discouraging moment to be the biggest encouragement for someone else. The most discouraging time of my life is when I found my courage!! My hope is when you read this book you will understand that regardless of the situation you face, there is an opportunity for you to be a courageous light for God and hopefully you will go out and allow your light to shine.

Genesis 50:20(NIV) You intended to harm me, but God intended it for good to accomplish what is now being done, the saving of many lives.

Be Strong